Around The Table

It's never too late to begin anew...

Dear Robin,

God bless you 2 !!!

This is my book in english.

I hope you like it !!!

Enjoy it ...

love in Him

gal 5:22-23 (Anna ♡)

4
28
20

MW01484152

AROUND THE TABLE
– It's Never Too Late to Begin Anew...
Copyright © 2016, 2019 by Anairam Góes Fernandes. All rights reserved.

No part of this publication may be reproduced, stored in a retrieval system, or transmitted in any way by any means – electronic, mechanical, photocopy, recording, or otherwise – without the prior permissions of the copyright holder, except as provided by USA copyright law.

Despite the author's desire to relate the historical portion of the story as accurately as possible, she will not be held responsible for the absolute certainty of all the information within this book. The author and the publisher will not be held responsible for any errors within the manuscript.

Scripture quotations marked NKJV are taken from the New Kings James Version. Copyright©1982 Thomas Nelson. All rights reserved.

Published by: Anairam Góes Fernandes

ISBN: 978-0-578-22549-4

Library of Congress Registration
Fernandes, Anairam Góes | Anna Goes
Around the Table
Registration Number: TXu 2-025-904 | August 04, 2016

Category: Marriage | Family | Christian Living

Written by Anairam Góes Fernandes | Anna4Jesus@hotmail.com

English translation by Laura Gequelin

Edited by Laura Gequelin

Cover Design by Isabel Gequelin

Cover Remastered & Text Layout by Eli Blyden |
www.EliTheBookGuy.com

Printed in the United States of America | Tampa FL |
A&A Printing & Publishing | www.PrintShopCentral.com

I dedicate this book to all women, no matter their age, culture or nationality, that want to live a life as part of a married couple with more passion and blessings, pleasure and happiness, loving and being loved.

It doesn't matter what challenges you face...
Don't give up your dreams.
It's never too late to begin anew...

Around The Table

Table of Contents

Foreword

"There you go again with your papers…"

Always writing something, huh?"

"I think it's time we clean up this office and throw some of these papers away."

These were just some of the things I said throughout our 40 years of marriage.

I could never imagine that one day, all of these scribbles, papers, and notes would come together into this book. In fact, if it wasn't for her insisting that we kept this immeasurable treasure of facts and stories from our life together, none of this would have been possible.

Today, I understand all the writing: God has a purpose for Ana to bless others through our lives. That's why, even today, she continues to keep notes on our lives, our relationships, our joyful moments and our troubled ones, our gains and our losses… as well as everything else that happens in our day-to-day.

And I truly believe that very soon, there will be enough material for the birth of a new book.

But in all of this, I just want to publicly profess my admiration and my respect for determination in turning the dreams God put in her heart into reality.

I'm sure this book, which is not based on a perfect marriage, but on respect, balance, and most importantly, love, will serve to help and guide those who need it.

Congratulations on your book, Ana!!!

May God continue blessing your mind and your heart!!!
I love you...

– Your husband, Marcelo Fernandes

Purpose

When I began writing this book, I was sitting on a chair at the edge of the beach beside my sweetheart, who was fishing on the island of Sanibel, Florida.

This book was written with the intention of helping couples have a happier and more gratifying life together.

God's plan for married couples is that they love one another in such a way that their lives become an inspiration for others to build their own families, primarily in the lives of their own children.

Marriage is a union in which we must have our minds set on making one another happy.

When you give up other things for the sake of love, your victory is on its way.

May God complete His purpose in your life as a couple.

Be blessed and victorious in Jesus Christ!

Around The Table

Thanks

I want to thank my Creator, my Savior, and the Holy Spirit who inspired me by giving me words when at times they failed me.

Thank you to my husband, my love, and companion: the gift God gave me who has helped me in all the phases of this book. I wrote, but he spent hours and hours by my side at home, correcting the book with a dictionary and at times, even inserting more adequate words and expressions.

I am grateful to my two children, who have helped us learn many things in our day-to-day lives since they were born.

Thank you to my father, who taught me values, and from whom I also learned to safely guard the things that we learn, write, and receive.

Thank you to my mother, a strong warrior, decisive and perseverant, who is always ready to help those in need.

Thank you to my grandmother, Laura, who passed away at 101 years old, but was always there for me in all the phases of my life.

Thank you to my grandfather and grandmother, Gozinho and Zilu, because I know that who I am and my walk with Christ is the fruit of their prayers.

Thank you to my assistant Isabel Gequelin for her help and support.

Thank you to Jennifer Tabora and Sandra & Roni for your beautiful photo on the cover of my book.

Thank you to my granddaughter, Laura Gequelin, and my daughter-in-law, Ingrid Fernandes, for helping me translate this book into English.

Thank you to my grandchildren, Laura, Isabel, Benjamin, and Caleb, for making me laugh and filling me with pride every day.

I want to thank my family; each of them has taught me something.

Thank you to all of you who, in some way or another, contributed to this project. May God bless you and repay you with all types of spiritual blessings.

It's never too late to begin anew...

by Anairam Góes Fernandes

Around The Table

CHAPTER 1

A Couple's Union Must Be the Priority

"Each is so close to the next that no air passes between them."

— Job 41:16

Amarried couple must have constant, frank dialogue. How can a person really know another person and have intimacy with them without spending quality time together?

We know couples who have been married for many years, who have celebrated 25 years together, 50 years together, and even more without ever so much as looking in each other's eyes, not even when they are talking to one another. They spend their entire lives like this...

There is something special about looking into the eyes of your spouse. It is a relationship so profound that you begin to know what your mate is feeling or thinking. It is a feeling of love, communion, and security. Intimacy is when you can say to your spouse, "I am here at your side. You can count on me."

One day, I heard that when you glue two pieces of paper together and then try to separate one sheet of paper from the other, the result is a disaster. They tear into various pieces. It is like this in a relationship between a man and a woman: they get married, make vows and promises before spiritual or civil authority, in front of family and invited guests, to live for one another in whatever circumstance, until death separates them. But when they can't resolve their differences with one another, the result is also ***disaster***.

The two leave the relationship broken and wounded. Yet society still claims that this is normal. That is all deception, that there is a natural tendency for a hurt person to injure others, to always put up a defensive attitude, and to give up trying another time because a sequel to the past relationship would be too hurtful to bear again.

The children of these unions are those that really suffer from divorce. Both my husband and I are children of parents who separated, and I cannot help but sincerely say that we suffered very much. There was so much hurt that it made us think and rethink about our own marriage choices. That suffering gave us a strong desire to persevere in continuing our own road together, even in the most difficult moments and great challenges for us as a couple.

I would describe marriage like this:

- *It is a life with daily challenges for the couple*
- *We must live one day at a time*
- *Each day is a gift, in that God grants us the breath of life, health, and the strength to work and overcome each obstacle.*

"Therefore, do not be anxious for tomorrow; for tomorrow will care for itself. Each day has enough trouble of its own."

– Matthew 6:34

Live each day with excitement, joy, and determination... for these days will never return again. Don't allow the obstacles and difficulties of life to impede you from being joyful and pleasant in all areas of your life.

Smile! For God has given a life for you to live with quality. He deeply cares for you and for your family. There are and always will be problems and difficulties, but solutions also come at just the right time.

When it looks like there is no solution, that's when God goes into action!

Each day is a gift from God. Jesus says,

"ANYTHING is possible to he who believes."

– Mark 9:23

Have a grateful heart and thank God for everything He has done in your life and in the life of your family. And also, don't forget to be thankful for your spouse. Think of how many people would like to go to sleep and wake up with someone at their side, to have someone to listen to them.

Why is it that the human tendency is to see the not-so-good side? Be happy you have a spouse. Look at all the blessings that the Lord has given you and all of what He represents in your life.

Gratefulness is a beautiful attitude that gives pleasure to the heart of your Creator. If you don't have a grateful heart, ask God in prayer to teach you to understand gratefulness and to thank people for the small things they do for you.

Let's change the subject just a little bit. It is written in Genesis 3:16,

"...your desire shall be for your husband..."

One day, a friend questioned me if a woman is not having sexual desires for her husband, can she go to God in prayer about this? I responded,

"Of course, you can! God is our Father, Creator, and Counselor."

— Isaiah 9:6

Many times you may think that your friend might be able to help you, but you must be careful with whom you share your intimacies.

I cannot neglect to emphasize that there are clinics and professionals out there to help in cases that require medical attention, but when the problem is just a lack of desire, many times, prayer resolves it all! A lack of desire can simply be fatigue, worry, stress, heartaches, or wounds (an important subject we will discuss in a later chapter).

If we can pray to our God for healing, salvation, deliverance from addiction, or finances, can we not also pray that He Himself would heal the hearts and lives of couples? He formed us, and He knows every cell of our body. He is our ever-present help in times of need. He is our refuge. We rely on Him!

Our life is a little box of surprises....

It is like a jigsaw puzzle wherein each piece fits perfectly until it forms a complete design.

Do you remember your wedding day? All the details, your ideas, and dreams coming to life.

And what about that to-do list, so that not one detail would be overlooked?

- *The dress*
- *The ceremony*
- *The reception*
- *The invitation list*
- *The honeymoon*

It didn't even matter where your honeymoon would be: a simple hotel or a luxurious resort, in your city or in another state, even in another country, a friend's house on the beach or on a ranch. Your goal was still the same: to be together with your loved one. It was like a dream, like you were somewhere in the clouds, right?

But when you return to *real life,* the commitments return, work and responsibilities all begin, with bills to pay and a home to take car, and so on. Now begins a period of adaptation, and the success of this really depends on if you are going to live as two separate individuals or together, as a family.

The two individuals will get to know each other more intimately, learning to live with the differences between them.

Speaking about our own experience, we got married very young and immature, without the necessary "planning ahead." But it was our decision, and even though our parents tried to alert us to the potential problems, we still persevered because we were confident in our decision.

The beginning of our marriage was very difficult and tumultuous. We lacked financial stability, which was a great burden on us, but we overcame the obstacles.

In Ecclesiastes 3, it is written:

"There is a time for storms, a time for refreshment.
There is a time to plant, a time to harvest.
There is a time to embrace, a time to refrain.
There is a time to laugh, a time to cry."

A couple's future is a product of these "times," so we must never disregard the beginning phase of a married couple's life together.

Today, when we look back at our start, we realize how much time we lost with silly little fights and nit-picking; however, this was all a part of our growth and maturing as a couple.

After years and years of living together, we often stop and notice how funny it is that we have the same thoughts, ideas, and goals, and it seems like one is reading the other's thoughts. Do you know what this is? It is *intimacy*, spending time with each other, truly fulfilling the concept of that "the two shall be as one flesh."

Everything in life needs a solid base to be built on, a sure and strong foundation.

Do you know why God created marriage? Because He Himself declared:

"It is not good for the man to be alone. I will make a helper suitable for him."

– Genesis 2:18

God wants us to feel secure with each other, and He wants to teach us to receive His council and guidance in all of life's circumstances. For, He is our secure harbor and our lighthouse.

The wedding ceremony lasts just a few minutes, but having a good marriage takes a whole lifetime of learning.

The Word of God says in Ephesians 5:22-33,

"Wives, submit to your husbands as to the Lord. For the husband is the head of the wife as Christ is the head of the church, his body, of which He is the Savior. Now as the church submits to Christ, so also wives should submit to their husbands in everything. Husbands, love your wives, just as Christ loved the church and gave Himself up to her to make her holy, cleansing her by the washing with water through the word, and to present her to Himself as a radiant church, without stain or wrinkle or any other blemish, but holy and blameless. In this same way, husbands ought to love their wives as their own bodies.

He who loves his wife loves himself. After all, no one ever hated his own body, but he feeds and cares for it, just as Christ does the church –for we are members of his body. For this reason a man shall leave his father and mother and be united to his wife, and the two shall become one flesh. This is a profound mystery - but I am talking about Christ and the church. However, each one of you also must love his wife as he loves himself, and the wife must respect her husband."

I have already personally experienced the two ways of living: being submissive and not being submissive. But I would counsel you that being submissive is more gratifying. There are things in life that one can't explain; you just have to live it to understand.

By stating this, I am in no way saying that a woman must not have any of her own opinions and ideas. It's not this at all, but it is walking beside your husband, being a loving, well-fit cooperator and collaborator together with him. Even if you are a very successful professional in your area, earning good money, fame, or stature doesn't matter when it comes to being submissive to your husband.

Do you know that when we make decisions in agreement with each other, things take a much more favorable course? For example, in raising children, buying large items, the administration of the finances, and in many other areas, being in agreement and harmony actually changes the course and the outcome of the decisions made.

"Again, I tell you that if two of you on earth agree about anything you ask for, it will be done for you by my Father in heaven." Matthew 18:19

Husbands also must have a heart ready to serve, for every true leader needs to know how to serve.

Nowadays, women work more, and when they arrive at home, they need their husband's help in preparing dinner, helping with the children's schoolwork, and everything else!

Happy women make their husbands happy, especially at nighttime…

A wife is a companion to her husband and not a competitor running against him.

There are couples who compete as to who earns the most money. But this is not healthy for the couple's relationship. It really doesn't matter who is more successful or earns more.

A couple together will do better than one person alone.

Let's look at *Ecclesiastes 4:9-12,*

"Two are better than one, because they have a good return for their work: If one falls down, his friend can help him up. But pity the man who falls and has no one to help him up! Also, if two lie down together, they will keep warm. But how can one keep warm alone? Though one may be overpowered, two can defend themselves. A cord of three strands is not quickly broken."

One day, my husband said to me, *"It gives me pleasure to give you pleasure."*

When a man and a woman make the decision to get married, they must, first of all, have the desire and mind-set to "make the other person happy." The fruit and harvest of having this attitude is guaranteed, and I can prove this!

Make good use of the time you have, dear wife; once you miss an opportunity, you can never get it back. And don't miss these opportunities…

- *A kiss is never too much*
- *A compliment pleases anyone's heart*
- *A phone call can lend sweet words*
- *A card can be given for no reason at all*
- *A comforting snuggle in an unexpected moment*
- *A sweet embrace can lead to good things*
- *…. and much more*

(*I'll let you put your imagination to work!*)

Together, we learn how to have a successful marriage. Men love to be valued: never criticize him in front of other people (I'll talk more about this in another chapter). Women appreciate gestures and words of love. No woman can resist this. Love and commitment grow when we walk together with these attitudes.

In the real world, we hear people saying that they don't want to get married.

There could be various reasons why: maybe they lived in a home where there was fighting and discord, or perhaps they had friends whose marriages were real failures. But the reality is that marriage doesn't depend on one only person, but on two.

With one persevering + the other one persevering = the two will overcome together and achieve their goal: a successful marriage.

Around The Table

CHAPTER 2

You Were Chosen

"Now the king was attracted to Esther more than any of the other women."

— Esther 2:17

Many times we see a couple and we think, "She is too pretty to be with him" or vice-versa, according to society's concept of beauty, and we cease to forget that none of that matters when you love.

In reading the story of Esther, we can see that the previous Queen was an attractive and beautiful woman. And the other women competing for the attention of the king were also certainly beautiful, but Esther had something different about her: a special spark. She was obedient, and she left a good impression on people.

Many times I have asked myself, how is it possible that two individuals with completely different backgrounds can fall in love and happily endure life together for several decades?

They begin to like the same things, the same television programs, and even sports that the other loves, therefore appreciating things that previously meant nothing to them.

One of the priorities every couple should have is to please one another, rather than pleasing everyone else around you.

Married life is filled with surprises, and every day brings something new.

Life as a couple is not always sunshine and flowers, but there are pleasant moments that are really unforgettable. And when we go through these difficult moments, we can refer what is written in Ecclesiastes 7:14,

"When times are good, be happy; but when times are bad, consider: God has made the one as well as the other. Therefore, a man cannot discover anything about his future."

We need to learn to live in those highs and lows of a relationship. It is like a gear that has an exact time to turn and connect with the other gear. Your relationship as a couple will come with the good and the bad. We simply cannot allow the good things that come our way to pass us by.

Don't leave for tomorrow what can be done today. When your spouse invites you to go somewhere or to do something together, do whatever you need to do so you can go with them; because just as the wave of the sea comes and goes, opportunities for moments together pass by.

There are moments that mark our lives in such a profound way that the couple never forgets them... as when you experience your first encounter, exchange looks, butterflies in your stomach, that first song that you hear together, your first kiss, the clothes that you wore, the first gift, and so on...

Looking back at the first things I wrote... is he still number one in your life?

Always remember those moments that have marked your lives: breakfast without the kids, a trip to celebrate a wedding anniversary, a walk together on the beach or in the country... I'm sure that you could make a list of great moments that you have shared with your loved one.

Give more value to the small things.

One encounter *"Around the Table"* is a chance to change circumstances and situations and once your opportunity is gone, you cannot go back and try again.

The King loved Esther very much, just as a husband should love his wife. God has plans for the man, the woman, and for the couple as a family. The man was created to be the provider and protector of the family.

When women began to claim the rights of equality, things began to change.

I could never say that women shouldn't study, work, get ahead in school, or contribute to the success of the family, because I have always worked and helped my husband. Even so, we can't forget the man is still the leader of the household, the priest of the family.

The long years that I have walked with the Lord Jesus, I have perceived a difference in the families who live their lives according to the Word of God and those that do not.

The first miracle that Jesus did happened at a wedding. Jesus transformed water into wine. It was at a wedding that Jesus revealed Himself as God the Provider and where He brought into existence something that didn't exist before.

Marriage is an institution created by God. It is the uniting of a man and a woman with different personalities, two different individuals, but with the same purpose: to <u>be happy together.</u>

But I want to ask you a question beyond this - do you want to be happy in your marriage? Then, make the other person happy. Beyond any shadow of doubt and without variation, whoever plants, reaps the harvest.

- *Plant tomatoes, reap tomatoes*
- *Plant okra, reap okra*
- *Plant love, reap love*
- *Plant understanding, reap understanding*

I want to say concerning our lives, that I have truly lived each day powerfully reaping this harvest. Many times what you want is different from what he wants. But it's better to recognize this today, in the here and now, for you will find everything to be more gratifying and compensating.

Waiting – I know it isn't very easy, but it is possible.

We need to learn every day that things are not always the way we want them to be, but they are the way they must be.

One day, my God really spoke to me that I needed to change my attitude. And I had thought that the person who needed to change was Marcelo! I was deceived on my part, and when I changed my attitude I could see a change in him also.

No one person can change another person.

Our partner is not an object in our hands, like a little remote control car that you can command the actions of where you want it to go.

People are created by God as individuals; there aren't two people exactly alike even though they may have the same desires and ideas.

God created each person on this earth for a specific purpose. That person is the only one who can interfere with whether or not his destiny will be fulfilled.

It's never too late to start or restart something new in our lives.

It doesn't matter what you already experienced or suffered in your relationship; it is possible to make changes in your attitude and behavior.

There is always a solution!

Jesus is the compass for whoever is without direction.

Maybe you have been lost in the middle of the sea waiting for help, feeling hopeless. If so, I want to tell you something very important: the boat has just arrived with Captain Jesus and He is inviting you to come aboard the boat with Him.

How amazing it is to be in a boat that is being guided by one who knows the course and direction to take. Waves come from one side and from the other, the storm is straight ahead on the horizon, and it rocks and shakes our boat, but the Captain continues firmly and securely at the command of the rudder and wheel.

The Lord wants us to have peace that exceeds all understanding, even in the midst of the storms of life.

"And the peace of God, which surpasses all understanding, will guard your hearts and minds through Christ Jesus."
– Philippians 4:7

When everything seems like there is no solution, Captain Jesus enters into action.
You can't change your spouse, but God can...
Pray and wait.

Many times, we may say that there is no resolution to our situation, but your testimony and behavior as a woman of God has astonishing results.

Ask your Loving Father to reveal to you what you need to change to better please your spouse.

God speaks, God reveals.

You are certainly the Queen Esther your husband loved more than any other woman. You are the favorite and the chosen one.

What a wonderful privilege. Rejoice in your heart, darling.

CHAPTER 3

Compliment Your Spouse in The Presence of Others, but Correct One Another Alone

"Through wisdom a house is built, and by understanding it is established."

— Proverbs 24:3

It's not easy when you encounter a situation in which your first impulse is to respond to a criticism you've received, whether it has a foundation or not.

Almost always, when there are arguments between two people, both think they are right, with each of them having their own excuses and ways to prove their point of view.

In a legal judgment, there are two lawyers: one for the defense and one for the accusing party. Both think they have the truth; for this reason there is a judge and a group of jurors to decide on what is the truth.

But with a couple, the cause must be resolved between them. Of course it should be emphasized that in some cases, it is necessary to incorporate the help of capable people to council them.

Criticizing or correcting in the presence of other people can cause great anger in the life of the accused. And many times it takes an unexpected direction of great proportions, and it can become almost impossible to undo the damage.

On the contrary, it is very gratifying and a wonderful feeling to be complimented by your spouse, just as much when you are alone as when you are in the presence of others.

You can never have too much: Compliment, compliment, compliment!

We must plant good things to reap in the future. Complimenting makes a difference, softens the attitude, and changes the heart of your loved one, and you get the victory!

I love complimenting my husband, children, grand-children, family members, friends, and all those that God has put into my path.

Words of encouragement transform lives!

I have had tremendous experiences of seeing lives completely transformed and healed by positive words that they have received. It has nothing to do with the power of the mind, but it is the power of the Word of God that makes this difference.

Imagine a person that was born and grew up in a family that only heard negative and defeating words about their lives. For instance, you will never get ahead in life, you will never amount to anything. Imagine always hearing this, how would you feel?

A wounded person wounds others. They don't have love to offer because they have a devastated heart, so they are always on the defensive.

When you touch the wound of a wounded animal trying to help it, the reaction is to try to strike at you, to hurt you, or even kill you.

Instead, change your circumstances by doing exactly the opposite, and maybe even use the "Around the Table" exercise. Praising one another only produces good things and it is never too late for God to transform a person's life. Do you want to know something? No matter how violent a person is, when Jesus enters their heart, their wounds are healed. This person becomes teachable, guidable, sweet-tempered and lovable; so much so that sometimes others don't even recognize them!

God has called people to help others be healed and restored, but only in the pure and true love of God do they have this ability. We must be instruments of love to others: to love is not only talk and give counsel, but it is touching the other person at the point of their need and supplying their necessities.

If a person needs a doctor, it doesn't really help to give them clothes. If they need food, it doesn't help at all to offer shoes. Try to have discernment as to what the person truly needs.

If someone is stingy or gives grudgingly, you need to provoke and encourage that person to give: give gifts to them and never forget to appreciate and thank all that they do... your attitude can change their behavior.

Words like:

- *You are special*
- *God has created you for something special*
- *God has a plan for your life*

- *You are more than a conqueror in Christ Jesus*
- *You are a blessing in my life*

Use the talent and potential that God has given you.

Yes, God will change them! I am real proof of that. God has transformed me and healed my emotions. Today I am a different person… with limitations but with hope that each day I live better and am happier than the day before.

God is the Magnificent and Sovereign King!

Words of encouragement are like fertilizer for your growing relationship, and will help the relationship flourish and mature, whether it's between a couple, family, or friends.

It is my hope that our testimony can strengthen your life and bring a time of new blessings: happier with your loved one and happier in the presence of our Lord Jesus Christ.

CHAPTER 4

Surprise Your Spouse

"Whatever your hand finds to do, do it..."
— Ecclesiastes 9:10

Many years ago when I still lived in Salvador, Bahia, in Brazil, Marcelo had been working outside the city, and it wasn't planned for him to return that night; to my surprise, he showed up in the middle of the night. That wonderful surprise marked my life, and I still remember it after so many years. It was an unforgettable night, and we both loved in a special way that day.

Sometimes Marcelo arrives home early from work without letting me know, and this still makes me happy. Even after all these years! Love renews itself each day.

Small things make my heart happy, and they mean a lot to me. At times, my husband arrives home with something for me: a soup that I like, a special tea, or even a piece of chocolate. I remember when one day, close to our first Christmas here in America, he came home with a little diamond ring with an engraving that said "I love you." I was so happy, and I still wear the ring to this day.

Many times, my husband arrives from work and I am all ready for us to go out to our own *"Around the Table."* It's not important where; it could be a little café, a restaurant, or the seaside. Use your imagination. But I am certain that it doesn't really work if you just stay home.

After God worked in our lives *"Around the Table,"* we haven't forgotten to practice this in our personal relationship either. It has helped us over three decades of marriage.

We are always going out with our kids or with other people to a restaurant or to the beach... but we never disregard our time together as a married couple. This is very important and has made quite a difference in our lives.

We have our own encounter *"Around the Table"* at least once a week. It works better if you two clarify the best day and time. It could be breakfast, lunch, or dinner... it just shouldn't be going to the movies, the theater, or anything that includes other people.

Spend time with the person that you have chosen to live with "until death do you part" - remember that oath you made?

When you spend time conversing with your spouse, you tend to get more and more acquainted each day. But don't forget one important thing: never share with anyone the weaknesses that your spouse reveals to you. No matter what happens, be trustworthy and keep these things in confidence.

I have already mentioned this before, but a good part of this book was written beside the beach on Sanibel Island, Florida. Whenever my husband went fishing, I would accompany him:

he would do what he liked to do and I would too, often reading and writing. Many times we would leave the beach with fish all ready to be cooked or baked. It is such a joy... our kids, grandkids, other family members, or friends come to our house and it all becomes a party!

What precious times! What awesome communion breaking bread together, living each day to its fullest... for today will never come again.

I know that there are couples who think they are too busy to take time for the "small" things, but your spouse and family, in the eyes of God, are much more important than even the "big" things. It is these small things that make your relationship so great and so joyful.

> *"Who despises the day of small things?"*
> – Zechariah 4:10

Some people choose a life with most of their time being spent apart from the other with the purpose of having enough money and power to enjoy material things, even if it comes with a marriage of little worth or bad quality. Married, but distant from each other: this is not worthwhile. I'm not talking about relationships where both of you have agreed to spend a determined amount of time apart for a certain goal or plan.

There are other cases of couples that delay their arrival at home in order to avoid seeing and conversing with their spouse. It may seem sad or odd but it's absolutely true.

But I have good news… it is never too late to begin anew! You may think there is nothing more that can be done, and maybe that's true for you, but for the All Powerful God that we serve, there are endless possibilities. It is He who can do great feats and change any circumstance!

"God is our refuge and strength; an ever present help in time of trouble."

– Psalm 46:1

When there is no other solution, that's when God comes into action.

Surprise your spouse… there is still hope.

Most of you already know that many women love shopping. I confess that I go shopping with my granddaughters, Laura and Isabel, or with my nephews, Alex and Gabriel. I always want to buy something for them. With the younger grandkids as well as with the adolescents, I make our outing into an *"Around the Table"* time. I love taking them out to pizza or some restaurant, and we enjoy just conversing about the important subjects in their lives.

I would like to mention something very important: when I am with Marcelo, sometimes I go shopping in a store that is of no interest to him, and he sits, waiting for me; I do the same for him when we're at his store. Marcelo enjoys hunting and fishing stores that are so huge that one could spend hours searching through it all to find everything that they want. I just find a bench to sit on, then read or write, maybe look at the big aquarium that they have in the center of the store, or just walk around with him being his companion. This system works for us... discover yours.

I want you to understand that as a couple, we cannot just do what makes *ourselves* happy, but we have to do what makes the other person happy too.

When we plant... we know for sure that we will reap.

As my grandfather, João Góes, always said, ***the planting is optional but the harvest is mandatory.***

Use the opportunities that you have!

Change the way you act... surprise your spouse and reap the good fruit.

The practice of ***"Around the Table"*** resolves situations and helps you make your decisions.

You know your spouse more than anyone. What can you do to surprise them?

- *Prepare breakfast early in the morning, so that afterward you can enjoy a little time...*
- *Leave them a note with an intimate message that only you two can know...*
- *Plan a surprise trip with the bags all packed...*
- *Go on a little drive to the place where you first met...*
- *Give them a balloon with something special written on it...*
- *Flowers or chocolates...*
- *Tickets for a show...*
- *And much more*

I am not talking about expensive gifts, but rather I want you to understand that you can be happy with what you have, and put your imagination to work. Your financial condition is important, but it's not everything.

There is a certain time for everything...

A few months ago, Marcelo arrived home one day and said, "Pack our bags because we're going on a trip to just have fun."

We traveled by car and we visited places like St. Augustine, Sarasota, and a gorgeous beach called Siesta Key. When we arrived there, it was already late in the afternoon; the weather was cool but the water was still warm and quiet. We had such a nice time swimming and having fun together. I loved that day.

Adventures like taking off on a little trip without previous planning or without reservations in a hotel is part of my personality. I like living like this, but sometimes my husband doesn't think this way. So we have to do things both ways, and try to please each other.

We are different but we can still make each other happy!

Many times Marcelo and I like to go out in the late evening to see the sunset at a pier near our house. If it's winter, we'll buy a coffee and in the summer, an iced tea. We sit on the bench and talk, kiss, and just have a moment of tenderness. These are some of the unforgettable moments as a couple. Sometimes we walk a little on the beach, enjoying the waves, the people passing by, kids running around, people fishing just for fun, beautiful yachts and little boats passing nearby the dock, and people with their metal detectors.

We need to appreciate the things around us whether it involves spending money or not. God created the sky, the clouds, the sea, and the sun; all these things affirm the existence of our Creator. You don't need to spend a lot to admire them.

Make time to be together.

Easy, simple moments of joy:

- *A quick trip to the store or bakery*
- *A walk on a trail or in a park*
- *Organizing the garage together or another part of the house*
- *Going to the dentist or doctor together*

Around The Table

CHAPTER 5

He Can Know Your Weakness

*"Therefore confess your sins to each another, and pray for
one another so that you might be healed..."*
— James 5:16

It happened one night at a pizza parlor. We had been
going through some difficult moments in our
relationship, and Marcelo even came to the point of
mentioning separation and divorce. I prayed to God and I
know that He was the one who gave me this strategy: we
needed to have an encounter ***"Around the Table"***. Many
times we need to take pause and put things in their correct
places before moving forward.

- *Dialogue changes circumstances*
- *Prayer changes circumstances*
- *There is a certain time for all things*

We must take that attitude when we feel that our home is
in danger, that we simply cannot leave things to crumble

away and collapse. Women are the backbones and backbones have to remain fixed on the spot, with a well-established foundation. Be a prepared person by reading books and participating in seminars and conferences regarding relationships.

An idea came to my mind, so I bought a little notebook and on one page, I made two columns. In one column, I wrote the qualities of my husband and on the other, I wrote his faults. I then spoke with Marcelo about my idea and he agreed to make his own list. We then just waited for each other to finish, and to our surprise, the list of the good qualities far outweighed the list of weaknesses.

What did we learn? That the enemy of our souls-the devil-wants to make us see the exasperating, irritating, infuriating weaknesses of our spouse. But these things are infinitely minor.

I want to assure you that an encounter "Around the Table" can change your life.

Our "Around the Table" God does feats of valor!

A change in attitude can change your life.

I am not just referring to the relationship between a husband and wife, but to any type of relationship. There are moments in our lives that we have to stop, and think before we act. We can't just let our lives be taken in whatever direction.

Life does not have a rewind button… what has passed, has passed.

Let's stop and think: what can we do to change our relationship?

God has given me many opportunities to grow and mature. I have learned to respect others' boundaries... those that I love and those who are around me.

We as parents, friends, and family can give council and direction, but we don't have the power to make a decision for someone else or just force them to do what we think is right. Each individual has their own free will given to them by God.

My rights end when I mess with the free will of another person, and vice versa.

While on the subject of parenthood, I remember what an adventure it was when our children arrived: our Janaina and little Marcelo. Those were precious times: giving the baby a bath, dressing them in cute clothes, nursing my babies, each one cuter than the other... it was all a joy. And then their daddy would arrive from work, and only have eyes for his little princess and little prince. It's a beautiful time where our house is full of new things.

But there are also the challenges: sleeping becomes a luxury, having to waking up through the night to feed the baby.

I need to emphasize something very important while on this subject. I have always had a husband who helped me a lot with my children and in all the phases of their lives, even nowadays when they are married. And I thank God for that because I know I couldn't have done it alone.

Good parenting is a lifetime job.

Now that the couple doesn't have all the time in the world to dedicate to each other anymore, where does that leave them? You can't wake up and go to bed at your own will.

You can't take the weekend off just to relax and watch TV or a movie without interruption? And let's not even talk about trying to fit in some alone time... because it is like their cue to start crying. Everything changes, right?

But it's at exactly this phase that this couple need the most love, selflessness, and understanding from each other... especially from the man to the woman, because she is going through so many changes in so many areas of her life.

- *A time of watchfulness*
- *A time to care for new members of the family*
- *A time of remembering that your spouse is important*
- *A time of new responsibilities*
- *A time to talk more than before*
- *A time of more tenderness with one another*
- *A time of growth as a couple and as a family*

This is the time to build on the good, strong foundation that we have laid, a time for the couple to conduct themselves as columns, well-driven into the foundation that is Jesus Christ.

> *"When times are good, be happy; but when times are bad, consider: God has made one as well as the other. Therefore, a man cannot discover anything about his future."*
> – Ecclesiastes 7:14

It is a time of to be alert and to invest in each other's lives.

Don't have reservations; openly confess your weaknesses to your spouse. After all, is there anybody better to do that with than your own flesh? This is the person with whom you have chosen to share the good things as well as the not so good.

"For this reason a man must leave his father and mother and be united with his wife, and they will become one flesh."
— Genesis 2:24

The two of us walking united together is more powerful than just the one. Jesus is with us to help, guide, and strengthen our union. When my husband is sad, I make him happy and he does the same for me.

"Though one may be overpowered, two can defend themselves. A cord of three strands is not quickly broken."
— Ecclesiastes 4:12

If you want to learn a little more about wisdom, read chapter 7 of Ecclesiastes.

It is so beautiful to see a man or a woman living for God with wisdom, a person who knows how to give counsel, acts with caution, and doesn't speak foolishly.

"My dear brothers, take note of this: Everyone should be quick to listen, slow to speak and slow to become angry."
— James 1:19

There is a saying in Brazil that says "If counsel were any good, it would be sold." This isn't true; good, wise counsel can change the trajectory of a life, of a city, or even a country.

We need to be sincere, truthful, and transparent with our spouse. If you are thinking about something that you would like to have changed, say it with love and kindness! Your spouse doesn't have the power to guess what you are thinking; you have to express yourself clearly.

Sincere communication between a couple is important.

I have heard stories of couples that separated over not being sincere with each other, even in the smallest things. They had never sat down together ***"Around the Table"*** to share their burdens, regrets, or even their joys with each other.

No one can read another person's mind.

Don't be immature, believing that if you share your weaknesses or faults with your husband or wife, they will take advantage of the situation against you. But believe that the other person is sufficiently mature to hear you and help you in these things. Often, whoever is on the outside of situations may have a different view and see an easier and clearer way for it to be resolved.

I remember when we went to a resort in Miami, the swimming pool had a slide where the kids could go down and then splash into the pool. Laura, our eldest grandchild, was about 6 or 7 years old at the time, and this was a big challenge for her. Finally, she decided to follow the advice we had given her and try it. She tried it, liked it, and just like that, she lost her fear. To our surprise, she didn't want to stop going down the tube. A little while ago, we were all at a water park and she went down this very high tube, without any hesitation.

We, in the same way, live through situations that we absolutely cannot find a solution to, but when we share it with our spouse, the situation resolves itself so quickly that it seems surreal. At times I have so many things to do that I don't even know where to begin, but then I talk to Marcelo who has a different angle on the situation, and I'll get an idea and everything gets resolved.

Do your part and wait for the solution to come.

My husband is a natural counselor and always has an advice to give. And when he doesn't know what to say, he responds "I'll think about it" and after a while, he shares his opinion.

We can learn about our role as a woman in Proverbs 31:10-31, which speaks about a wise woman:

"A wife of noble character who can find?
She is worth far more than rubies.
Her husband has full confidence in her
And lacks nothing of value.
She brings him good, not harm,
All the days of her life.
She selects wool and flax
And works with eager hands.
She is life the merchant ships,
Bringing her food from afar.
She get up while it is still dark;
She provides food for her family

And portions for her servant girls.
She set about her work vigorously,
Her arms are strong for her tasks.
She see that her trading is profitable,
And her lamp does not go out at night.
In her hands she holds the distaff
And grasps the spindle with her fingers.
She opens her arms to the poor
And extends her hands to the needy.
When it snows, she has no fear for her household;
For all of them are clothed in scarlet.
She makes coverings for her bed;
She is clothed in fine linen and purple.
Her husband is respected at the city gate,
Where he takes his seat among the elders of the land.
She makes linen garments and sells them,
And supplies the merchants with sashes.
She is clothed with strength and dignity;
She can laugh at the days to come.
She speaks with wisdom,
And faithful instruction is on her tongue.
She watches over the affairs of her household
And does not eat the bread of idleness.
Her children arise and call her blessed;
Her husband also, and he praises her
Many women do noble things;
But you surpass them all.
Charm is deceptive, and beauty is fleeting;
But a woman who fears the Lord is to be praised.

Give her the reward she has earned,
And let her works bring her praise at the city gate."

The Lord gave me marvelous grandmothers. My Grandma Zilu was a warrior and a wise, faithful servant of the Living God. She cared for her household, feared God, and had a great influence on my life. My Grandma Laura had her own special way to help me in anything that I needed and always gave me good advice.

This has helped me become a wise grandmother and an example to my granddaughters, Laura and Isabel, and to my grandsons, Benjamin and Caleb. I know they love me and they are loved by me just as I was by my grandparents.

CHAPTER 6

You Love Your Descendants, but You Are One Flesh with Your Spouse

"For this reason a man shall leave his father and mother and be united to his wife, and they will become one flesh."
— Genesis 2:24

We have two kids: Janaina and Marcelo Jr. Janaina is married to Marcio, who have given us our precious granddaughters, Laura and Isabel. Marcelo Jr. is married to Ingrid, who was pregnant with our first grandson when I wrote the first draft of this book, our sweet Benjamin and another beautiful grandson, Caleb.

My love and I are very blessed with our descendants.

"Their descendants will be known among the nations and their offspring among the peoples. All who see them will acknowledge that they are a people the Lord has blessed."
— Isaiah 61:9

We must be cautious in our attempts to resolve situations between our children. We as parents cannot side with one or the other, not defending or speaking against any of them.

Sometimes we know who is right, but I prefer not to give my opinion. When we say that one of them is right and not the other, no one is left satisfied.

Some parents show their preference for one of their children. In the Bible, Isaac and Rebecca did this and caused damage to their family and to humanity in general. However, I believe that some parents and children identify with each other more in terms of personality, manner of thinking or behaving, or maybe even liking the same things.

When we come across a situation that needs to be resolved in the family, I let my husband, Marcelo, take the lead. My husband is a wise and prudent counselor. Of course we make mistakes, but more often we are correct. There are days where I wish there weren't ever arguments or disputes between children or the parents. Unfortunately, this happens in every family.

I advise you to listen to everything each of them has to say but NEVER take sides. Children are a blessing and a gift from the Lord that make our hearts glad…

Especially the grandchildren. Right, grandmas?

"Sons are a gift from the Lord, children a reward from Him."

– Psalm 127:3

Remember this: every child is unique and different from the other, with different qualities, weaknesses and personalities. Our love for each one of them must be equal, even if you don't agree with their behavior and their choices.

Love is commanded by God, even toward that child that gives you the most trouble and keeps you up at night... Accept them with love; however, this does not mean that you are agreeing with their actions and errors.

Plant love... whatever you plant, you will reap.

God created each of us to do something special on this earth. Are you fulfilling your calling? It doesn't matter if it is known or seen by others; the important thing is to do the will of your Creator. He is a God who gives each one of us a specific calling of what He wants us to do.

Sometimes, we love to get off track or try and embellish what God has instructed us to do. If God told you to make pasta, don't go out and make lasagna!

Maybe God has chosen you to be a successful professional, but as you fulfill your calling, don't forget your obligations as a wife, mother, and administrator in your household. God might have called you to be an intercessor for those in need, or maybe have a ministry with children. Perhaps no one else is seeing what you do but God is always watching... and the result is always extraordinary.

"See to it that you complete the work you have received in the Lord." Colossians 4:17

We women were created to be wives, mothers, professionals, and much more. All these things have their time and place for actualization. Being a wife is a very important role in the family. Have you ever observed that when we are at peace with our husbands, everything else goes well in the other areas of our lives? Do you know why? It's because we are one flesh with our spouse; this is a partnership created by God that we cannot explain or understand.

At times, I am busy doing something and Marcelo calls me and asks me to do something for him; I think to myself, "Should I go now or just wait and do it later?" When I think of going right away, I know it's the right thing to do, and many times I'm surprised with something good.

Please your husband and great things will happen...

Today, after over forty years of marriage, we share the same thoughts in so many situations, desires, and dreams. The hand of God has been so beautiful and faithful in our marriage. Just as it has happened between the two of us, it can happen in your marriage between the two of you.

I must be honest though; in the beginning of our relationship, in those first few years of marriage, it wasn't all lovely and enjoyable, but it was worth waiting for the harvest. I am extremely happy with the husband that God has given me and with the family that we have built together.

It's true that your spouse needs to have a place of priority in your life... but do not take this to an extreme. When the babies arrive, they take up a lot of the mother's energy and time. During this phase, it can become quite difficult to spend time together as a couple. They need to maintain an attitude of understanding and, of course, lots of love. If you have a second child, once they arrive, things fall into place easier, since you already have some experience from the first child.

This is a time when the couple can't just stop and make love anytime they want to… Often the baby cries as soon as you start, then you have to stop everything because the mood is ruined.

As a couple, it is necessary to have structure in your relationship, with a firm commitment to one another in order to overcome the obstacles and difficulties.

Like everything in life, books, retreats, and seminars on the subject of marriage and raising children are all part of the necessary preparation and education.

Time passes quickly and children grow. Soon, they can play alone and watch movies by themselves. It is in this time that the couple begins to have more liberty to be alone and take an hour or two to themselves as they like.

And who says that that a moment of love-making has to be at the quiet of the night? Routine can turn even enjoyable things boring!

When your children become adolescents, you have to be careful, especially if you have a curious daughter like mine. Even if sometimes you just have to put on some music to not allow any sound to escape for them to hear.

Then your children get married and the grandchildren come. The house is full and your hearts are too, with the delight of being grandparents! Don't lose any opportunities; live each day to the fullest with your spouse, children, and grandchildren.

Live with enthusiasm! Enjoy the moments! Focus your life on the good and pleasant things, on the day-to-day adventures.

Problems, difficulties, and losses will pass and are overcome as life goes on.

It's not worthwhile living a life with your spouse that has more sad moments than happy moments. Arguments are at times inevitable, but be careful not to argue in the presence of your children. Spare them the pain of hearing those destructive words said between the two of you.

"Do not let the sun go down while you are still angry."
— Ephesians 4:26

A couple must never go to bed hurt or angry with each other.

Marcelo and I have made it a point to never go to bed angry with each other. This would happen often before we were saved, but now that we have received Jesus Christ as our Savior, we have a whole new outlook; we are learning each day to act in a different manner.

We must develop good habits like:

- *Kiss each other and your children when you come and go*

- *Be thankful for everything that one does for the other (and the kids too): a cup of water, a surprise gift, a chocolate, flowers, or maybe even jewelry. It doesn't matter the value... be grateful!*

- *Call during the day to say a loving word, like: I love you; you are important to me (we need to say these things to our children, as well).*

- *Travel as a family to a beach house in the summer, a cabin in the winter, or another place of your preference.*
- *Unite the family with a special breakfast, lunch or dinner on a daily basis or for commemorative dates.*

My love leaves very early to go to work and even if I don't wake up, he'll come to my side of the bed and gently kiss me. This isn't just a ritual. He still does it even if I don't see it and I'm sound asleep.

Just remember that the practice of being *"Around the Table"* is very important in all the family encounters.

Why say negative comments if positive comments are the ones that are truly important?

In a certain year of her adolescence, our daughter, Janaina, had difficulties in school, and she wasn't improving in the way she needed. The Lord gave me a strategy to help her; I would pray and confess God's word over her life in a loud, declarative voice: "Janaina likes to study and she is an excellent student, in the name of Jesus!" Today we see the fruit and reward of these prayers. She really did turn into an excellent student; so much so that one of her professor at her college here in the United States cited her work as an example in the classroom. She also recently graduated with her Master's degree in Nursing Anesthesia! Her primary language is not even English, but Portuguese. So this is a result, not just from her mental strength, but from the Word of God, that when confessed, generates response!

"If you believe, you will receive whatever you ask for in prayer."

– Matthew 21:22

God is the One that changes the circumstances. It is enough for you to simply believe.

At times, you need to stop your activities to help your children through a difficult phase, when they encounter challenges that will be overcome with help from their parents.

Our son, Marcelo Jr., in my perspective, has never given us many problems. He didn't talk a lot; he had good discernment. He is quite the counselor and always gives good advice. He speaks little and observes a lot. However, during one period of his adolescence, he needed me to dedicate more time to him, caring for him in a close and special way.

"Everyone should be quick to listen, slow to speak and slow to become angry."

– James 1:19

Ultimately, our children married quite early, as their parents did.

I am grateful to God for the opportunity to always be together as a family. Once in a while, we stay together until the early morning hours playing games at home. We go bowling together, go to the beach to watch the sunset, and of course, the occasional last-minute barbeque or our special dinners with typical Brazilian food. We like to transform all these occasions into happy moments.

Every encounter is unique and special. But the fellowship and communion are the most important of all these things. We speak and express what we feel, and it is so wonderful. *"Around the Table"* happens easily and naturally during these family times.

Around The Table

CHAPTER 7

Be Happy and Enjoy what You Have Even if You Desire to Have More

"How can I repay the Lord for all His goodness to me?"
— Psalm 116:12

There is nothing wrong with desiring to have something better even if you already possess it, whether it be a new car, a house, finances, or a ministry.

We must have short-term, mid-term, and long-term goals in our plans.

There are people that live their entire lives wanting the car of their dreams, but just sit around waiting for this happen. They never realize that it is necessary to invest time and work hard towards accomplishing their dream. Nothing happens by just waving a magic wand and your desire won't become a reality that easily. Don't forget that magic is just an illusion.

We must fight to achieve our victories.

The farmer aerates the earth, plants the seeds, waters his plants, and waits for the harvest. This process takes months or even years. Okra comes in quickly; pumpkin and squash take a bit more time, and a mango tree, much longer.

It is like this with our times of harvest.

The Word of God says in Ecclesiastes 3:1-11,

"There is a time for everything, and a season for every activity under heaven; a time to be born and a time to die, a time to plant and a time to uproot, a time to kill and a time to heal, a time to tear down and a time to build, a time to weep and a time to laugh, a time to mourn and a time to dance, a time to scatter stones and a time to gather them, a time to embrace and a time to refrain, a time to search and a time to give up, a time to keep and a time to throw away, a time to tear and a time to mend, a time to be silent and a time to speak, a time to love and a time to hate, a time for war and a time for peace. What does the worker gain from his toil? I have seen the burden God has laid on men. He has made everything beautiful in its time. He has also set eternity in the hearts of men; yet they cannot fathom what God has done from beginning to end."

What I often see around me is that there are people who never feel satisfied or happy with what they have, and spend their whole lives wanting what they don't have. At the end of their careers and their lives, everything that they did was done in vain. They lived a frustrated life without joy in what they had and ended without accomplishing what they really wanted.

It would have been better to come to the end of your life and say what is written in 2 Timothy 4:7,

"I have fought the good fight, I have finished the race, I have kept the faith."

Your emotional health suffers when you are always anxious about having what you cannot have, and many want to blame God for this.

There are other paths to getting what you want: receiving an inheritance, winning a drawing or a raffle, or something else unexpected... yes, life is full of surprises!

For you to have something of greater value, you first need to take care of what you already have.

How is it that God can present you with a growth in your business if you can't administer well what you already have? How can you gain a new home or a better car if you are not taking care of the one you have now?

First step: Do your part.

Experience will come with time.

A young person cannot have the same level of experience as an older person. There is a great difference between learning through studying books and learning through the experiences of life, acquired over many long years.

There are attitudes that can aid us in acquiring what we want like integrity, honesty, decision-making, and diligence.

However, in my life, I have witnessed people being blessed in different areas from their career to their finances to their goals. How many times have we thought to ourselves, "Why are they blessed?" We think that they don't truly deserve a blessing. We, being human with our egos and all, only see the outside. But read Matthew 5:45,

"He causes his sun to rise on the evil and the good, and sends rain on the righteous and the unrighteous."

Another important point is that God doesn't desire for us to be greedy and tightfisted, or squander and waste the provision of the Lord. You must take care of what you have.

<u>Organization</u> is very important in order to have a victorious life.

I have learned that there is always provision, oftentimes just under our nose, but we fail to see it. The first reaction you have when you need something is to go to a store or market and buy it; we go running, looking for what we need, when what we need has been in our home all along: in the pantry, the cabinet, or even the closet. God can provide in ways we cannot even imagine!

This can even occur with the nonmaterial needs in our life. We can travel to try and find happiness; we can look for love and affirmation from our careers and our studies; we can find our peace and identity from things that will leave us shakier than before.

This has happened so many times in my life. I confess that at the beginning of our marriage, I was not an organized person. I learned little by little. Of course, I need to mention that our daughter, Janaina, is one of the most organized women I know! She is a warrior and a winner in Jesus Christ.

The United States has been a great blessing in my life. Here, I learned to cook, care for my home, and so much more. Here, we learned to truly appreciate all the helpful things available for the home.

We have had several meetings, dinners, and gatherings for prayer in our home, both with friends or groups of women, and with Brazilians, Americans, and Hispanics too. It gives me such joy to prepare everything and afterwards, to clean it all up and put everything back in its place. Marcelo is a great partner in the food preparation. He helps me before and after the event, and always supports me in all the projects and in the purposes of God for my life. We know that together we fulfill the will of God.

"Around the Table" great things can happen.

In our family dining room, miracles have happened "Around the Table."

It is written in Matthew 21:22,

"If you believe, you will receive whatever you ask for in prayer."

"Around the Table," weighty decisions are made during family gatherings (even the presidency of a country).

"Around the Table," the division of personal goods happen, wedding dates are decided, lives are saved by medicine, careers are chosen, positions taken, and surprises of every type are revealed.

"Around the Table," the rules are decided and enforced.

"Around the Table," great things happen!!!

I want **"Around the Table"** to become something you practice often, to help you resolve what you need to have resolved. Don't ignore what needs to take place; don't just close your eyes and pretend that something is not happening in your life that needs to be dealt with.

Take a position today and don't leave it for tomorrow.

You can gain a great victory!

- *Is your soul feeling fulfilled?*
- *How is your relationship as a couple?*
- *Are you happy the way you are living?*
- *Do you want something better?*

Many times, a couple is just surviving in their relationship but this is never just what God desires for us. He wants us to enjoy the wonderful things in a marriage. Don't adjust to and become satisfied with a lackluster, lukewarm relationship, push beyond mediocrity to arrive at a marriage of quality and excellence. This is the plan of your Creator for your marital relationship.

Live each day looking forward to better days, because they are coming!

Seek to accomplish your dreams together with your spouse. Many times, they might be very similar, but have never really been discussed, explained, or talked about between the two of you.

- *Know that it's never too late for changes.*
- *Share your dreams.*
- *It is never too late to dream and achieve these dreams.*
- *Hope makes us believe in better days ahead.*

Right now, I am bringing into existence a big dream in my life: to write and publish my book.

Our dreams should please the heart of God and bring blessings to our lives and to the lives of others.

We know people who were graced by God with gifts, possessions and riches, and others who only have the means for survival. Why the difference? They could be part of the same family. God gives to whom He wants and what He wants. I learned one day that the prosperity of God is the absence of need.

I live today in a phase of my life where I no longer work like before. But I am fulfilling the calling of God for my life by helping prisoners to have a less difficult life, writing letters about my thoughts and sharing my experiences.

Always when I have needed something, this "something" arrives right in my hands. For example, I had needed a new printer, and my husband arrived home earlier than usual, took me to the store and purchased one for me. Then we went to our own *"Around the Table"*.

How great it is to serve a God that takes care of all our needs.

Be happy with what you have even though you desire more.

Around The Table

CHAPTER 8

God Does It ... Prayer Works!!!

"For nothing is impossible with God."

– Luke 1:37

It is written in the Word of God that there is a right time for everything. There is a proper moment to speak and reveal your thoughts and ideas. Prepare the right place, the right moment. It could be at a restaurant, café, or on the beach... but it's better to find a place away from home, your cell phones, and the kids. Nothing must interrupt this precious time.

An encounter like this can change many things. Here in the U.S., we call this a date.

Do you remember that story I shared with you earlier in the book? About the list of qualities we loved and those we didn't Marcelo and I made one night at a pizza place? Do you remember what we discovered after we completed the task?

The list of things we loved about each other was long, but the list of weaknesses was really short!

The enemy makes us see an ant as the size of an elephant. He shows us our problems with a magnifying lens and shows the solutions with a reduction lens.

When God enters into action, He transforms any situation.

Remember this: NEVER forget to compliment and thank your spouse for the many things they do for you. Don't neglect these things, for it is in the small details that we gain our victories.

When I gave my life to Jesus, I learned from a sister in Christ that we shouldn't take the problems that happen during the day and present them to our husbands the minute he walks in the door, tired from working. The better choice is to wait for a moment, maybe after he has taken a shower or eaten his dinner. When he arrives home, his head is still full of worries from his day, and it is necessary for him to relax and rest a bit. Otherwise, it will make his head swim! It seems to me that we women have the capacity to accumulate and manage many more activities and situations in our heads than men… there's just no other explanation.

Still today, though we have children who are already married and are now grandparents, I still do things this way; I wait for Marcelo to get home, take his shower, and eat dinner or a snack before I tell him about my day, the choices I made, and the situations that arose.

Sometimes it takes the right strategy and the right moment to prepare a person to receive certain news or hear about certain occurrences.

I need to emphasize something very interesting. After we were married, majority of the time, we disagreed on various things: subjects, attitudes, thoughts, likes, or dislikes. But today, after a long time journeying together through life as a couple, most of the time, we like the same things and appreciate what the other appreciates. This is most likely to happen when a couple chooses to deny themselves out of love and a desire to please the other.

One funny example that I always remember is that I actually learned to eat sushi because of Marcelo. When he used to go fishing, I would never like going with him. But today, that has completely changed. I appreciate going with him so much and at times, I am the first one to suggest that we should go fishing. I don't fish, but instead go just to keep him company. It's a time that I've decided to use for writing, reading, prayer, or sewing, while sitting in my beach chair. But the best part of all is, of course, being with each other.

Whenever I write a card of congratulations to a bride and groom who have just gotten married, the main idea I try to convey is summed up in the phrase: *"deny yourself."*

It is impossible for a couple to live well together without each one denying themselves many times of their own wishes. A relationship cannot function without self-denial.

In denying yourself to please your spouse, you will receive great rewards in exchange.

Imagine what it would be like if you denied yourself of your own will to please your loved one…

It is wonderful!!! It is awesome!!! It is gratifying!!!

Why would you want to be at odds with the person you have chosen, to whom you have said "I do," and promised to be faithful to in all circumstances of life until death do you part? You made a vow in front of the minister, your family, invited guests, and most importantly, before God... So, insisting on your own will just isn't worth it!

When we deny ourselves, we show real love.

> *"A gentle answer turns away wrath,*
> *but a harsh word stirs up anger."*
> – Proverbs 15:1

When we feel offended, our first reaction is to return what we have received. But it says just the opposite in Proverbs 15:1.

Some people speak or write whatever comes to their minds, without concern to the other person or the damages they will cause.

My advice is to do the absolute opposite: when you are injured by someone for whatever reason, let that initial anger pass so afterward, you can write or speak what is necessary in a calm and rational manner. Before you act without thinking, stop and reflect, because the Holy Spirit will surely guide you in the right way to change the outcome of the incident.

This isn't an easy thing to do, but we can learn.

Instead of saying: "You don't remember to do anything!"

Say, "You forgot about this but I know that next time you will remember."

Instead of, "You are such an aggressive person."

Say, "Don't you think your reaction is just a little harsh?"

Think and meditate before you act or speak.

The reaction of the other person could be positive or negative, all depending on the way that you say things. It will depend on your attitude.

"Love is patient, love is kind. It does not envy, it does not boast, it is not proud. It is not rude, it is not self-seeking, it is not easily angered, and it keeps no record of wrongs."
– 1 Corinthians 13:4-5

Remember that the Word of God is our guide and has the answer to every one of life's circumstance.

Around The Table

CHAPTER 9

Don't Share Your Spouse's Virtues or Weaknesses with Your Friends

*"And I will give them one heart and one purpose:
to worship me forever, for their own good and for the good
of all their descendants."*
— Jeremiah 32:39

There are situations that the couple goes through that God doesn't want other people to know about, things that are to remain only between the couple and perhaps the children.

One day, someone told me that a person who is your friend today could possibly not be your friend tomorrow. People change their ways of thinking and make other choices. The person you think is your friend could actually be jealous of you, wanting to replace you.

Don't share personal things with your friends that should have been left just between the couple. It is not wise or prudent to do this, for the only people involved are the couple themselves.

When I accepted Jesus as my personal savior, I learned that we must never speak badly of our spouse to others under any circumstance.

My Grandma Laura would always tell me a Brazilian saying that translates to something like **"dirty laundry is to be washed at home."**

What do you do if you discover the naked truth about your family, like the son of Noah did?

"Noah... when he had drank some of its wine, he became drunk and laid uncovered inside his tent. Ham, the father of Canaan, saw his father's nakedness and told his two brothers outside. But Shem and Japheth took a garment and laid it across their shoulders; then they walked in backward and covered their father's nakedness. Their faces were turned the other way so that they would not see their father's nakedness."

– Genesis 9:21-24

What would your attitude be?

In other words, this story has multiple layers for us to consider (more than just the literal). It is not right to speak openly of the private intimacies of a couple or of your family.

How many different yet serious problems can happen in a family? Adultery, fraud, drugs, fighting, and so on... Why should we speak to others about these things who are not even involved at all? Before you know it, that person you shared with talks to another person, and he talks to another, and he talks to another, and on and on it goes.

I am also referring to bragging about the things that your spouse does for you, for no particular reason at all.

It is easy to cry along with those in the midst of tragedy, losses, or death, but it is often the case that rejoicing in the victories of others is not always so easy.

Whenever I am in a situation where I feel a need for me to share my testimony, like the healing of my emotions, the restoration of our marriage, or the curing of cancer, I do it in order to help others have a better life and strengthen their trust in God.

I am going to repeat myself one more time: it is not wise to reveal and discuss those things that should not be spoken about. *BE CAREFUL!* Do so out of respect for your relationship as a couple, out of respect for your children, or out of respect for the person who revealed that secret to you, confiding in you as a friend.

As parents, in certain situations, we should know what is going on with our children, whether they are married or single. We as parents have a little more experience in life regarding many problems that they may be passing through, because we have often already lived through those problems in the past. However, remember that every little detail of every little thing does not need to be shared from parent to child nor child to parent.

PAY ATTENTION!!! Don't talk about your spouse, whether good or bad, for there are things that are only meant for the two of you.

"In the Lord, however, woman is not independent of man,
nor is man independent of woman."
— 1 Corinthians 11:11

Mary, the mother of Jesus, guarded in her heart the message delivered to her by the angel that she would be the mother of the Savior, who was to be called Jesus. She wasn't yet married to Joseph, so imagine what people would have said about her. How could she be pregnant and have a child without having intimate relations with a man? She kept the angel's message to herself, and she was victorious because of her attitude.

The result was extraordinary! She gave birth to a son who changed the history of the world, forgiving our sins and giving us eternal life! Choosing to speak at only the right time brings great benefits. What a blessing!!!

Now read Luke 1:26-38,

"In the sixth month, God sent the angel Gabriel to
Nazareth, a town in Galilee, to a virgin pledged to be
married to a man named Joseph, a descendant of David.
The virgin's name was Mary. The angel went to her and
said 'Greetings, you who are highly favored! The Lord is
with you.' Mary was greatly troubled at his word and
wondered what kind of greeting this might be. But the angel
said to her, 'Do not be afraid, Mary, you have found favor
with God. You will be with child and give birth to a son,
and you are to give him the name Jesus. He will be great
and will be called the Son of the Most High. The Lord God

will give him the throne of this father David. And he will
reign over the house of Jacob forever; his kingdom will
never end.' 'How can this be,' Mary asked the angel, 'since
I am a virgin?' The angel answered, 'The Holy Spirit will
come upon you, and the power of the Most High will
overshadow you. So the holy one will be born and will be
called the Son of God. Even Elizabeth your relative is
going to have a child in her old age, and she who is said to
be barren is in her sixth month. For nothing is impossible
with God.' 'I am the Lord's servant,' Mary answered. 'May
it be to me as you have said.' Then the angel left her."

Back to our first discussion, did you know that some
people become your friend just to gain information from you
and that in the end, it can be disastrous? There are also friends
who promise wise counsel but in the end, only make situations
worse. I'll give you an example: when a couple is going
through a difficult time, there are people around them that try
to "help them." However, their advice can often be horrible. I
have experienced situations like this. ***BE CAREFUL!!!***

Our responsibility is to unite ourselves as it is written in
Matthew 12:30. If you cannot contribute for the good of a
situation, don't give opinions, close your mouth, and don't
get involved in that which is outside the extent of your own
responsibility.

God built the family and does not take pleasure in its
division, like through divorce. Remember my illustration of
the pieces of paper, that when two pieces are glued together
then separated, both sides are now torn. This is like the heart

of a person who separates or divorces. Even though in the future they may rebuild a new family, the old scars are there permanently. They may forgive and the hurts may be healed, but the scars stay. The memory of suffering does not just disappear. It is only true that, with the passing of time, you remember a little less each day. Though you remember what happened and can still feel the scar, the deep suffering of that which is truly forgiven is much, much less.

It is written in Matthew 6:14-15:

"For if you forgive men when they sin against you,
your heavenly Father will also forgive you. But if you
do not forgive men their sins, your Father will not forgive
your sins."

If forgiveness is a commandment of God, whoever forgives or asks for forgiveness will be blessed. For it doesn't matter whether we *want* to forgive or not, or who is right or wrong in the matter.

I want to share with you something that happened in my life when I was a volunteer in a prison here in the United States. I worked with teenagers between 14 and 17 years old. Even though they were so young, many of them had committed horrible crimes. They had hearts already filled with hate, heartache, hurt, and resentment. As we as human beings often do, when they actually did commit a crime and were found guilty, they would try to put the blame on others. (However, I know they were driven to commit these crimes by "friends" or even family members.)

But what the enemy of our souls tries to do in these situations is help the guilty feel like they weren't responsible and avoiding facing or accepting their error, rather than seeing their error, repenting of it, and being healed.

I have witnessed these children with so much bitterness in their hearts, and I didn't know what to do to help them… Then I had an idea: for them to be able to really forgive, they would have to declare out it loud with their mouths. However, the boys rarely had even a moment alone where no one else could hear them… except for their shower time. So I began teaching them that whenever they took a shower and they were underneath the showerhead, with water falling over their heads and cleaning their bodies, to pray in this manner:

"Lord, just like this water is cleaning my body, help me cleanse my soul and my heart by forgiving _____ (repeat this as many times as needed). *I forgive* _____ (name of the person), *I forgive* _____ (continue repeating).

This should be done for as long as it's needed until the person is certain they have truly forgiven the person and the burden of anger and hate is off their shoulders. If you need to forgive, there will come a day in which God's bright light will shine in your life and you will feel free!

It says in Isaiah 10:27,

> *"In that day, their burden will be lifted from your
> shoulders, their yoke from your neck."*

This is what happens when you forgive. With the passing of time, the wound doesn't hurt any longer, and you suffer no more, even though the scar doesn't disappear, and occasionally it comes to your mind that it did happen.

Everyone goes through difficult times as a result of a divorce; the parents, the children, and everyone around them is affected.

It's like a vase that breaks; it's impossible to put all of the pieces back together, even if the pieces seem to easily fit together again.

If you are going through a situation like this, *pray*. Because the All-Powerful God who has formed you, created the skies and the earth, and has chosen you since you were in your mother's womb, is a specialist in restoring your life and renewing the love that you have lost.

Who can get in the way of Him working in your life?

He can cure your emotions; He is the Doctor of all doctors, and the Psychologist of all psychologists. He is perfect and He makes everything new; He brings things into existence just to bless YOU.

I must make it clear that in certain situations, it is necessary to have the help of a competent professional or the help of someone that God has put in our path to guide us. God always shows us a direction to take. He wants the very best for us.

"Therefore, if anyone is in Christ, he is a new creation; the old has gone, and the new has come!"
— 2 Corinthians 5:17

- *Call out to Him...*
- *Talk with Him...*
- *Search for Him with all your heart...*
- *Confess to Him your weaknesses...*

The ears of the Lord are always attentive to our prayers–whoever or wherever you are. Open your heart and talk to God about everything that you feel. You don't need pretty words, just a sincere and open heart.

Around The Table

CHAPTER 10

Don't Criticize the Family of Your Spouse

"For a son dishonors his father, a daughter rises up against her mother, a daughter-in-law against her mother-in-law - a man's enemies are the members of his own household."

— Micah 7:6

The Bible tells us that our enemies are our own family. My grandmother Laura used to quote a popular saying: ***Just like fingers on the same hand are different, children of the same parents are also different.***

Mothers, mothers-in-law, daughters-in-law: many times, they act jealous and possessive, but the truth is that each of them holds their own special place in your life. When someone is single, the parents need to be in first place in the life of that individual. However, when that person marries, things are very different. The spouse is now the one that occupies that space of priority, in order to complete that which is written in Genesis 2:24,

"For this reason a man will leave his father and mother and be united to his wife, and they will become one flesh."

Many parents don't take this seriously. When our children were teenagers, we always taught them this commandment of God for families. Today, they are married and have children, and I can see that they have learned this principle. I am grateful to God that we were able to minister this to their hearts. I believe that mothers have a lot of influence in the lives of their children: when they are little and also when they are married.

Sometimes, they want to think and act in their own way, and it's not easy to see some of the decisions your children make, which in your eyes, as parents who are presumably more experienced, may seem wrong.

We as parents learn from our errors in the same way as our children, sons-in-law, and daughters-in-law. As parents, we need to instruct them and guide them, but it is necessary for them to have their own experiences and important to know where to begin and end that influence in their lives.

If for some reason we are present when our children are in a discussion with their spouse, the best position we can take is to be neutral, not taking sides or giving opinions. However, we can pray and intercede before the Lord.

Whenever it is possible, we must take the time to advise and counsel them.

"The prayer of a righteous man is powerful and effective."
– James 5:16

This is an alert even for us as a couple that when there is a disagreement or discussion between the two of us, the best thing to do is for one of the two to close their mouth. Oftentimes, there would never be an agreement in that moment, but later, the situation can be resolved.

Marcelo and I decided to get married very early. We suffered resistance from both of our families. Like most, they thought that the best thing for us would be to wait, mature a bit, and be more established financially. Our parents were right, for we lived through great challenges, and yet we overcame them all.

Because of our experience, we understand that when young people decide to get married, it is difficult to get them to understand that it really is better to wait.

Maybe when you know and fear God and desire to obey and please your parents, you will come to accept the idea of waiting until the time is right. I think couples should follow this concept, but truthfully, who is going to hold down two young people who really want to get married? It is often difficult, but sometimes it is possible.

Marcelo and I had only known each other for a short time and somehow we already had a conviction of what we wanted: to live our whole lives together and to share every moment with each other. Like I already said, we faced many challenges, but thankfully we overcame them all.

Now think with me... how can a man, from a family that you barely even know, unite himself with a woman whose family he also doesn't know? Families with personalities, habits, and customs that are completely different from each other. Yet, you unite in marriage with your friends and family present, and go on to live your lives together... from sleeping together at night to waking up together in the morning to sharing what you have with the other. It is very interesting when we stop to think about it. There must be something supernatural on God's part in all this! It really is a beautiful thing.

When Marcelo and I got married, we didn't know this awesome God who we serve today. But He chose *us* and always protects us at the times that we need it most.

Life and Heart to Jesus

*Would you like to give your life and your heart to Jesus?
If so, repeat this prayer:*

Dear God,

I want to ask you for forgiveness for all of my sins, and give you my life, my heart, my decisions, and my future. I need your direction to help me make the right choices.

Jesus died on the cross to give me life and abundant life to the fullest.

I am grateful to you for loving me first and choosing me.

You did not choose me, but I chose you and appointed you to go and bear fruit – fruit that will last. Then the father will give you whatever you ask in my name.
—John 15:16

I love you, Jesus.
Amen.

Around The Table

About the Author

Marcelo and I were married very early while we were still young and immature.

We have two children: Janaina, who is married to Marcio, and the two have given us our precious granddaughters Laura and Isabel, and Marcelo Jr., who is married to Ingrid, who have given us two adorable grandsons Benjamin and Caleb.

We currently live in the state of Florida.

With more than four decades of marriage, we can share our experiences of overcoming many obstacles and conquering the difficulties along our path. Still today, we continue fighting and winning the battle so that we can declare each day that we are victorious through Christ, as a couple, as parents, as in-laws, and as grandparents.

All I have to say is:
Thank you my Jesus for everything!!!